Goodbye Dad

A TODDLER PREP™ BOOK

Ready SetPrep

Copyright 2022 ReadySetPrep LLC

Toddler Prep™, ReadySetPrep™, and associated trademarks are owned by and used under license from Phase 2 LLC.

All rights reserved. No part of this book may be reproduced or used in any manner without written permission of the copyright owner except for the use of quotations in a book review. For more information, contact author.

All characters and events are products of the author's imagination, and any resemblance to actual events, places or persons, living or dead is entirely coincidental.

Photo credits: © Shutterstock.com

About Toddler Prep™ Books

The best way to prepare a child for any new experience is to help them understand what to expect beforehand, according to experts. And while cute illustrations and fictional dialogue might be entertaining, little ones need a more realistic representation to fully understand and prepare for new experiences.

With Toddler Prep™ Books, a series by ReadySetPrep™, you can help your child make a clear connection between expectation and reality for all of life's exciting new firsts. Born from firsthand experience and based on research from leading developmental psychologists, the series was created by Amy and Aaron Pittman – parents of two who know (all too well) the value of preparation for toddlers.

Dad is very special. You love to be with him all the time. He makes you feel safe and happy.

You have so much fun when you're with Dad. You play games, cuddle, and wrestle.

And Dad *always* takes good care of you. He loves you so much.

But sometimes you have to say goodbye to Dad - just for a little while.

You might say goodbye to him in the morning when you go to school . . .

. . . or when he has to go to work.

Sometimes you say goodbye when he has to go to the store...

. . . or goes to the gym for exercise.

But no matter where he goes, Dad *always* comes back.

There are lots of fun ways to say goodbye. You can give him a big hug and kiss. I wonder how tight you can squeeze?

Or you can give him a high five or maybe even have a secret handshake.

Then, when it's time to go, Dad says, "Goodbye. I love you! I'll see you soon."

You might feel a little sad to say goodbye to him. It's ok to feel sad. Remember, Dad *always* comes back.

If you feel sad, you can give your favorite stuffed animal a BIG hug just like you would give Dad a big hug.

While Dad is gone, you can do so many fun things...

You can play with your favorite toys or even draw him a picture.

You can listen to music and do a silly dance. Show me your best dance!

Sometimes you might think about Dad when he is gone. Just remember, Dad *always* comes back.

And before you know it, he is back here to see you!

When Dad comes back, you can give him a great big hug and kiss! Hooray!

And he is so excited to hear about all the fun things you did. It's so nice to be with Dad.

Made in the USA
Las Vegas, NV
24 February 2025